9455
FIRE EXTINGUISHER INSIDE
9455
Trains
Heather DiLorenzo Williams and Warren Rylands
EYEDISCOVER

Go to **www.eyediscover.com** and enter this book's unique code.

BOOK CODE

AVY38575

EYEDISCOVER brings you optic readalongs that support active learning.

Published by AV² by Weigl
350 5th Avenue, 59th Floor New York, NY 10118
Website: www.eyediscover.com

Library of Congress Control Number: 2018953523

ISBN 978-1-4896-8335-9 (hardcover)

Printed in Brainerd, Minnesota,United States
1 2 3 4 5 6 7 8 9 0 22 21 20 19 18

082018
120917

Project Coordinators: John Willis
Designer: Mandy Christiansen

Weigl acknowledges Alamy and iStock as the primary image suppliers for this title.

EYEDISCOVER provides enriched content, optimized for tablet use, that supplements and complements this book. EYEDISCOVER books strive to create inspired learning and engage young minds in a total learning experience.

Watch
Video content brings each page to life.

Browse
Thumbnails make navigation simple.

Read
Follow along with text on the screen.

Listen
Hear each page read aloud.

Your EYEDISCOVER Optic Readalongs come alive with...

Audio
Listen to the entire book read aloud.

Video
High resolution videos turn each spread into an optic readalong.

OPTIMIZED FOR

- TABLETS
- WHITEBOARDS
- COMPUTERS
- AND MUCH MORE!

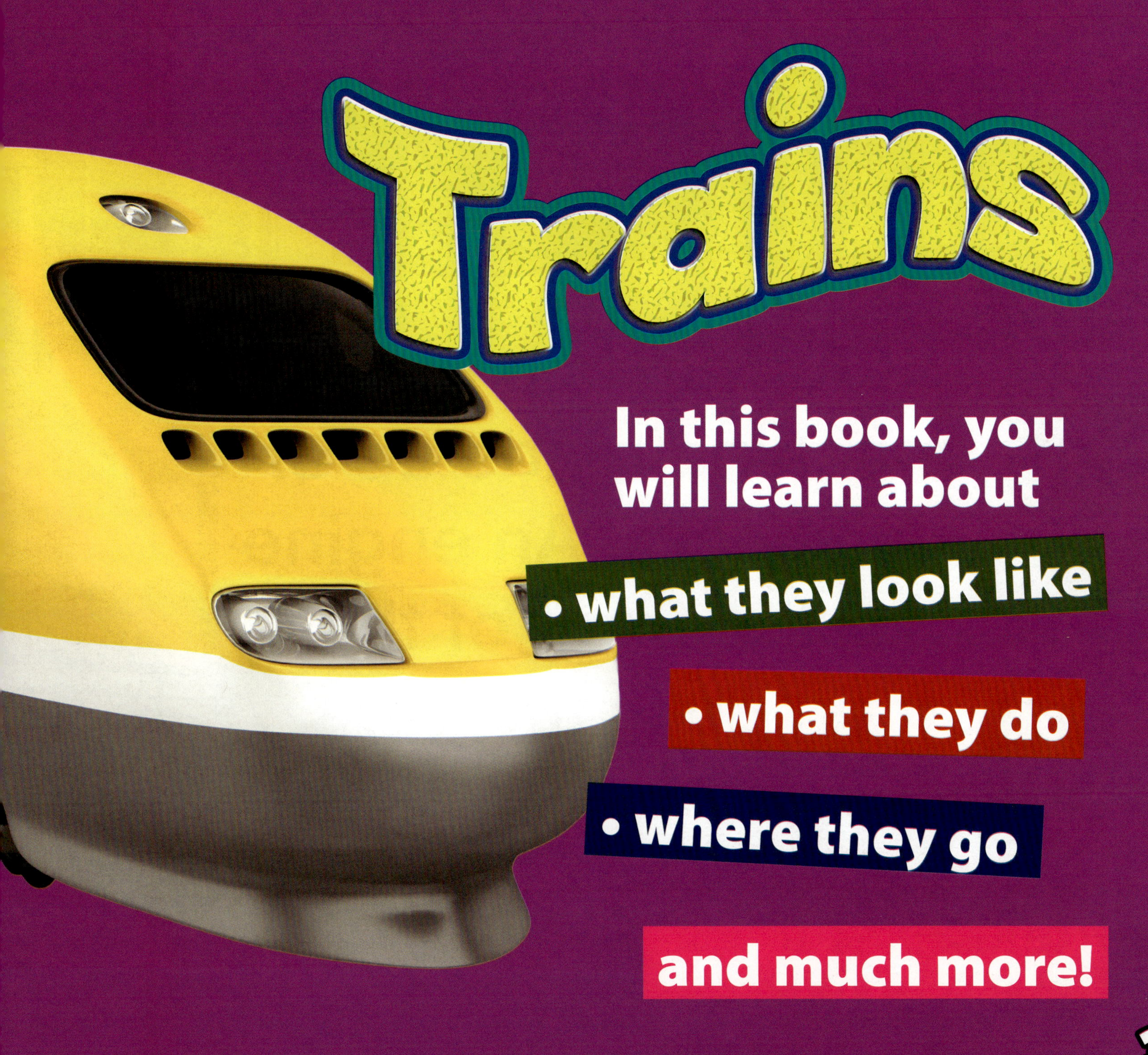

Trains

In this book, you will learn about

- what they look like
- what they do
- where they go

and much more!

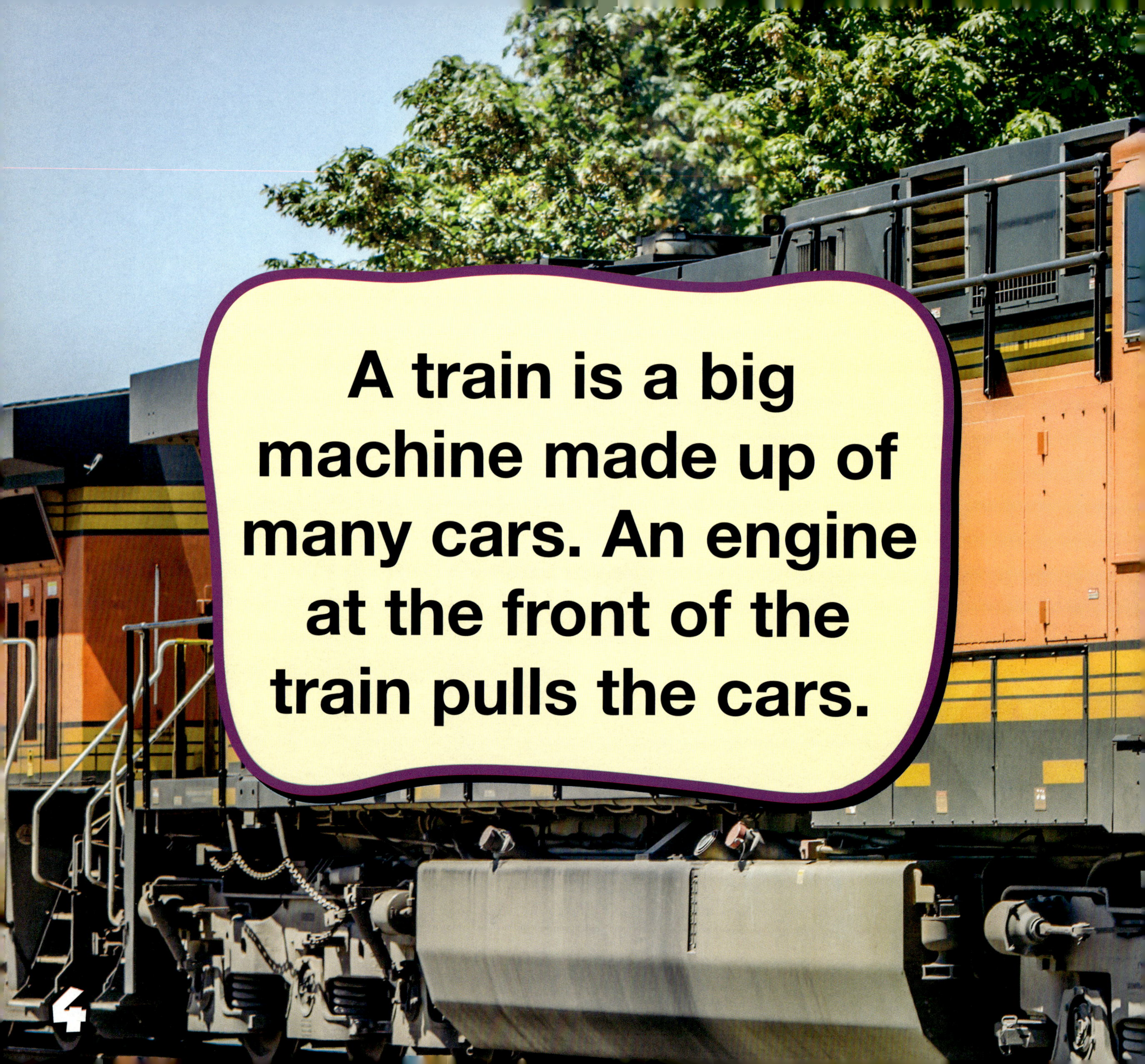

A train is a big machine made up of many cars. An engine at the front of the train pulls the cars.

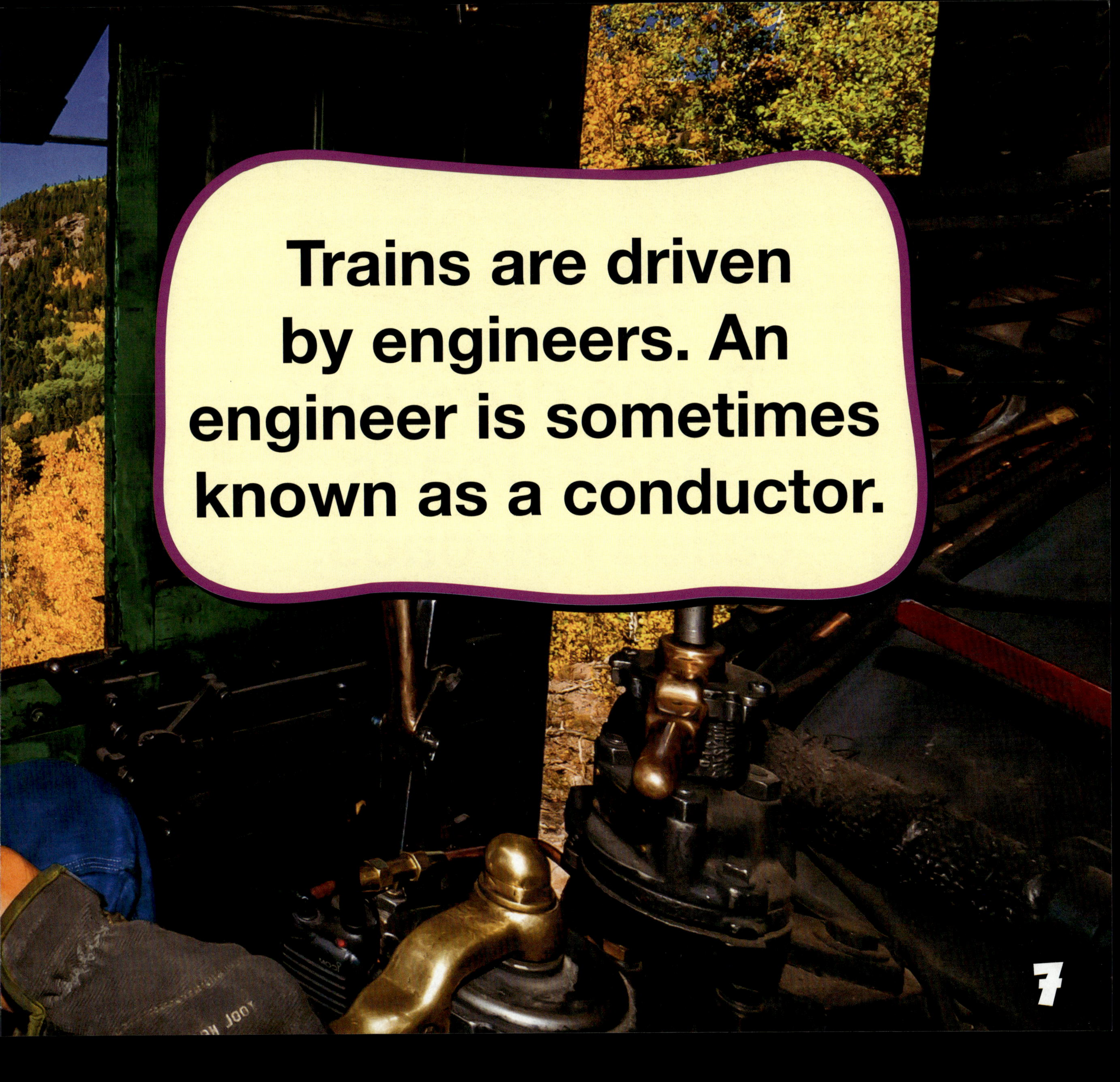

Trains are driven by engineers. An engineer is sometimes known as a conductor.

Trains drive on special roads called railroads. Railroads can also be called tracks.

25

MLN
29
506
UR
Queen Victoria
GWR

There are many different kinds of train engines. They can be powered by diesel, electricity, or steam.

Trains can be very long. They can have as many as 600 cars.

ScotRail
ScotRail
158720

There are two types of trains. Passenger trains carry people, and freight trains carry things people need.

The world's fastest train is faster than a race car.

Shin-ōsaka,Shin-kōbe,Okayama,Fukuyama,Hiroshima,Kokura
列車がきます。ご注意ください。
NOZOMI 9 9:30 Hakat
SOS
SOS

7
Please be advised that train doors will close 30 seconds prior to departure
First class

People go to a train station to travel by train.

Trains are a fun way to travel and see the world.

The **United States** has enough railroad tracks to circle **Earth**

five times.

The **Trans-Siberian Express** is the longest train ride in the world. It lasts

six days.

A man from **Great Britain** invented the world's first train in **1804.**

The **Channel Tunnel** is an underwater railroad track that is **31 miles** long. (50 kilometers)

The **heaviest** train ever weighed more than **99,000 tons.** (89,811 metric tons)

The **longest** passenger train in the **world** has **44 cars.**

KEY WORDS

Research has shown that as much as 65 percent of all written material published in English is made up of 300 words. These 300 words cannot be taught using pictures or learned by sounding them out. They must be recognized by sight. This book contains 39 common sight words to help young readers improve their reading fluency and comprehension. This book also teaches young readers several important content words, such as proper nouns. These words are paired with pictures to aid in learning and improve understanding.

Page	Sight Words First Appearance
4	a, an, at, big, cars, is, made, many, of, the, up
7	are, as, by, sometimes
8	also, be, can, on
11	different, or, there, they
12	have, long, very
15	and, carry, need, people, things, two
16	than, world
19	go, to
20	see, way, world

Page	Content Words First Appearance
4	engine, machine, train
7	conductor, engineers
8	railroads, roads, tracks
11	diesel, electricity, steam
15	freight, passenger
19	station

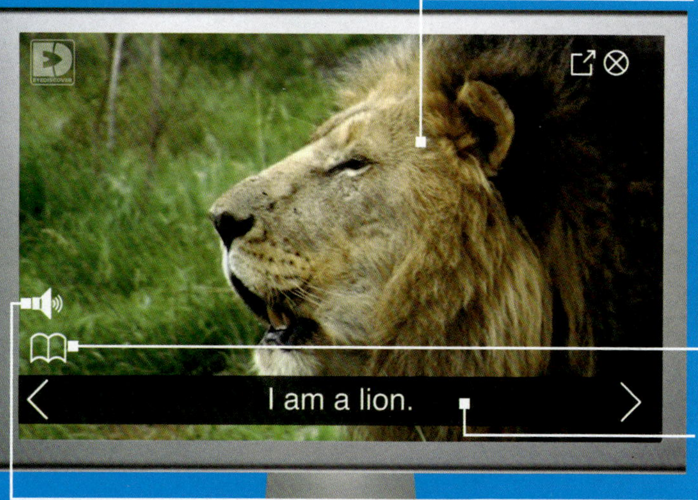

Watch
Video content brings each page to life.

Browse
Thumbnails make navigation simple.

Read
Follow along with text on the screen.

Listen
Hear each page read aloud.

Go to www.eyediscover.com and enter this book's unique code.

BOOK CODE

AVY38575